W9-AWN-031

WITHDRAWN

FAMOUS
LATINOS

Ellen Ochoa

First Latina Astronaut

Lila and Rick Guzmán

Enslow Elementary
an imprint of

Enslow Publishers, Inc.
40 Industrial Road
Box 398
Berkeley Heights, NJ 07922
USA
http://www.enslow.com

Series Adviser
Bárbara C. Cruz, Ed.D., Series Consultant
Professor, Social Science Education
University of South Florida

Series Literacy Consultant
Allan A. De Fina, Ph.D.
Past President of the New Jersey Reading Association
Professor, Department of Literacy Education
New Jersey City University

Note to Parents and Teachers: The *Famous Latinos* series supports National Council for the Social Studies (NCSS) curriculum standards. The Words to Know section introduces subject-specific vocabulary words.

This series was designed by Irasema Rivera, an award-winning Latina graphic designer.

Enslow Elementary, an imprint of Enslow Publishers, Inc.

Enslow Elementary® is a registered trademark of Enslow Publishers, Inc.

Library of Congress Cataloging-in-Publication Data

Guzmán, Lila, 1952–
    Ellen Ochoa : first Latina astronaut / Lila and Rick Guzmán.
      p. cm.
    Includes index.
    ISBN 0-7660-2642-6
    1. Ochoa, Ellen—Juvenile literature. 2. Women astronauts—United States—Biography—Juvenile literature. 3. Astronauts—United States—Biography—Juvenile literature. 4. Hispanic American women—Biography—Juvenile literature. I. Title.
    TL789.85.O25G86 2005
    629.450092—dc22

                       2005031743

Printed in the United States of America

10 9 8 7 6 5 4 3 2 1

To Our Readers:
We have done our best to make sure all Internet addresses in this book were active and appropriate when we went to press. However, the author and the publisher have no control over and assume no liability for the material available on those Internet sites or on other Web sites they may link to. Any comments or suggestions can be sent by e-mail to comments@enslow.com or to the address on the back cover.

Every effort has been made to locate all copyright holders of material used in this book. If any errors or omissions have occurred, corrections will be made in future editions of this book.

Illustration Credits: Ellen Ochoa, pp. 6, 7 , 12, 15; Grossmont High School (photo by Boyd Anderson), p. 8; NASA, pp. 1, 4, 16 (all), 17, 18 (both), 20, 21, 22, 23, 24, 26, 27, 28; Sandia National Lab, p. 14; San Diego State University, p. 10; Stanford University News Service, p. 11.

Cover Illustrations: NASA

❊ Contents ❊

Ellen played her flute in outer space.

1

Childhood

Flute music floated 160 miles above Earth. Inside the space shuttle *Discovery*, astronaut Ellen Ochoa was playing a song. Playing the flute in space was almost the same as playing it on Earth. There was only one difference. In space, the instrument and the pages of music floated. For Ellen, the most amazing part of all was looking down at the beautiful planet Earth while she played.

Ellen Ochoa was born on May 10, 1958, in Los Angeles, California. Her father's parents were from Mexico. They came to the United States before Ellen's father, Joseph, was born. Ellen's mother, Rosanne, was from Oklahoma. Ellen has a sister and three

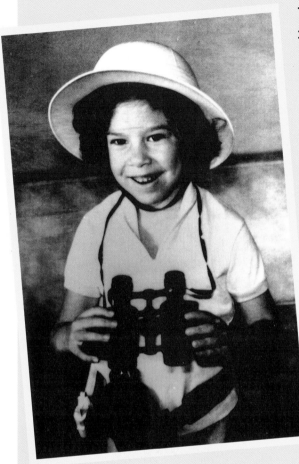

Young Ellen already looks ready to go exploring.

brothers. When she was little, her family moved from Los Angeles to La Mesa, a town near San Diego, California.

When Ellen was a year old, her mother started college. Most people can finish college in four years. It took Rosanne Ochoa twenty-two years because she took only one class at a time. She had five children and was very busy.

Ellen's mother was very interested in her college classes. She talked to her children about what she was studying. From her mother, Ellen learned that education is important and exciting. She learned to work hard and not to give up.

On July 20, 1969, American astronauts went to the moon. Neil Armstrong was the first human being to walk on the moon. Eleven-year-old Ellen watched it on television. It was amazing, but Ellen did not think about becoming an astronaut. At that time, all astronauts were men.

Ellen, age nine or ten.

In high school, Ellen's nickname was "E."

Ellen's parents divorced when she was in junior high school. Ellen and her brothers and sister lived with their mother. In high school, Ellen studied hard. She liked her classes in math and reading. She also loved music and played the flute in a youth orchestra in San Diego. In 1975, Ellen graduated from Grossmont High School in La Mesa. She was the top student in her class. She decided to go to a local college, San Diego State University. She knew how hard her mother worked as a single parent. She wanted to be close to her family so she could help out with her younger brothers.

2

Ellen Goes
to College

At San Diego State University, Ellen had to choose her favorite subject to study. She was interested in many things. She enjoyed music, math, English, and business. Finally, after she took a class in physics (FIZ-iks), Ellen made up her mind.

Physics is the science that studies matter, energy, and motion. It tries to understand why things look and act the way they do. How do rainbows form? Why do flags wave in the wind?

In 1980 Ellen received a degree in physics from San Diego State University. Once again, she was the

Ellen did an experiment in the physics lab at San Diego State University.

top student in her class. What should she do next? Ellen thought she might like to get a job playing the flute in an orchestra. Yet there was still so much that she wanted to learn about science. So Ellen became a student at Stanford University. It is one of the best schools in the country. This time, she wanted to study electrical engineering.

Electrical engineers create machines that use electricity in new ways. They may design computers or computer programs. They may work on lasers or robots and invent all kinds of new things. While Ellen was at Stanford, she did research in optics—the science of light. Ellen helped invent a special optics machine that could "look" at objects and inspect them for mistakes.

Ellen earned two advanced degrees in electrical engineering from Stanford University. In 1981 she received a master of science degree. Then, in 1985, she finished her doctorate, or Ph.D. This is the highest college degree. People who earn it are called doctor. Ellen became Dr. Ellen Ochoa. She made perfect grades at Stanford and graduated at the top of her class. She also played the flute with the Stanford Symphony Orchestra and won the Student Soloist Award.

While Ellen was in college, women were permitted to to be part of the

The engineering building at Stanford.

Ellen and her proud family after she was awarded her Ph.D. in 1985.

space program for the first time. Now a woman could be an astronaut for NASA (the National Aeronautics [air-uh-NAW-tiks] and Space Administration).

In 1983 Sally Ride became the first American woman in space. Because of Sally Ride's success, Ellen saw that it was possible for anyone to become an astronaut. She decided she wanted to be one, too.

3

Becoming an Astronaut

Ellen applied to NASA's astronaut program in 1985, but she was turned down. Instead, she started working at Sandia National Laboratories. There she did more research in optics. In 1988 she took a job doing optics work for NASA's Ames Research Center. At Ames, she was in charge of a team of thirty-five scientists. She was the co-inventor of two more inventions. One of them made robots able to "see" objects. This would help robots move around in a spaceship or in space. The other invention made pictures taken by cameras in space look clearer.

At Sandia National Lab, Ellen worked on optics research.

Ellen still hoped to join NASA's Astronaut Corps. She knew that many astronauts are pilots and can fly airplanes, so she took flying lessons. She earned a pilot's license in 1986. She applied to NASA again in 1987. But again she was turned down.

At Ames Research Center, Ellen met Coe Fulmer Miles. He was a research engineer, too. They fell in love and were married on May 27, 1990.

Ellen was busy and happy with her job and her new marriage, but she did not give up on her dream. In 1990 two thousand people applied to become astronauts. Only twenty-three were selected—and Ellen was one of them. She was the first Latina accepted into the NASA astronaut training program.

Ellen earned her pilot's license. Here, she stands with her friend John Curley.

Astronaut training offers lots of new experiences—on land, in the water, and in the air.

Astronaut training took place at the Johnson Space Center in Houston, Texas. Ellen had to work very hard. She had to be strong and fit. NASA taught the new astronauts what it felt like to be in a space shuttle. They learned what to do in any kind of emergency. Ellen practiced jumping out of an airplane with a parachute. Ellen also had to study the earth, the ocean, and the stars. New astronauts had to become experts on the space shuttle and how it works. They had to know every inch of it, inside and outside. After months of hard work, Ellen became a U.S. astronaut in July 1991.

The new NASA graduate.

The
FUEL TANK
and
ROCKET BOOSTERS
launch the
shuttle, then
fall back
to Earth.

SPACE
SHUTTLE

The space shuttle blasts off like a rocket, but it lands like an airplane.

4

Blasting into Space

On April 8, 1993, Ellen went on her first space mission, aboard the space shuttle *Discovery*. The trip lasted nine days. The astronauts on a space shuttle do many experiments while they are traveling around Earth. Ellen helped gather information about how the sun changes the climate on Earth. She used a robotic arm to send out a satellite to learn more about the sun. Then, with the robotic arm, Ellen brought the satellite back inside the space shuttle.

For her second flight, Ellen spent twelve days on the space shuttle *Atlantis*, November 3–14, 1994.

Ellen and her son Wilson in 1999.

Scientists wanted to learn more about the energy of the sun. Ellen again used a robotic arm to catch a research satellite at the end of its eight-day flight.

Ellen's son Wilson was born in 1998. He would celebrate his first birthday while his mother was on her third shuttle mission. Before she left, Ellen made a videotape of herself for Wilson to watch every night at bedtime. On May 27, 1999, Ellen took off for ten days on the space shuttle *Discovery*. It had an international crew. Members of the Canadian Space Agency and the Russian Space Agency went with American astronauts.

On May 29, the space shuttle docked with the International Space Station. The crew was excited to be the first space shuttle flight to dock with the station.

The International Space Station is a place where humans can live and work in space for long periods of time. It was built by people from sixteen countries. The first crew would arrive at the space station in 2000.

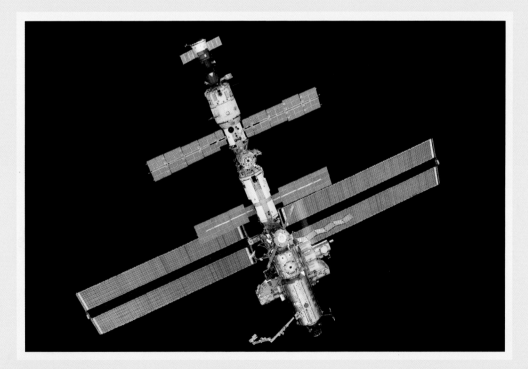

This photo of the International Space Station was taken by an astronaut on the space shuttle in 2002.

Ellen floats through a tunnel from the shuttle to the space station.

Ellen and the other astronauts helped get the space station ready. They moved medical equipment, clothing, sleeping bags, extra parts, and water from the space shuttle to the space station.

They delivered about four tons of supplies.

On April 8, 2002, Ellen went on her fourth trip into space. She and the crew of the *Atlantis* returned to the International Space Station. Ellen used the space station's robotic arm to help astronauts walk in space. The arm held on to them as they moved around outside the space station. This was the first time the arm was used this way.

This astronaut is being held by a robotic arm.

Inside the shuttle, Ellen works the controls of the robotic arm.

The shuttle brought along a new section to add to the International Space Station and make it bigger. The space shuttle also delivered more science experiments, laptop computers, water, and other items the astronauts needed on the space station.

By the end of her fourth mission, Ellen had spent nearly one thousand hours in space.

5

Ellen Ochoa Today

Dr. Ellen Ochoa has won many awards for leadership, for service to the space program, and for her work in space. She has also been honored by many Latino groups. She is still an astronaut for NASA and would be happy to go into space again. For now, her job is on the ground. She works at the Johnson Space Center in Houston, Texas. She has been in charge of the crew working on the International Space Station. Another of her jobs is to decide which astronauts will go on different space flights.

In her free time, Ellen likes to ride her bicycle and play volleyball. She also enjoys playing the flute and flying small airplanes. Ellen and her husband, Coe, have two sons: Wilson, born in 1998, and Jordan, born in 2000. Being a mom and an astronaut keeps Ellen very busy.

On the shuttle, Ellen can work upside down. When she is not in space, she keeps her feet on the ground.

Ellen Ochoa can remember a time when there were no female or Latino astronauts. By 2006 there were thirty women in the Astronaut Corps at NASA, as well as thirteen Latinos (all men, except Ellen).

Ellen travels all over the country. She enjoys talking to children and adults about the space program. She visits schools to talk to the students. She encourages them to take classes in math and science.

Ellen tells everyone to work hard and follow their dreams.

Ellen believes that exploring space is very important. It will take people to new worlds. "Don't be afraid to reach for the stars," she says. "I believe a good education can take you anywhere on Earth and beyond."

Ellen hopes more young people will choose to work in the space program.

✳ Timeline ✳

1958 Born on May 10 in Los Angeles, California.

1975 Graduates from Grossmont High School in La Mesa, California.

1980 Earns a degree in physics from San Diego State University.

1981 Earns a master's degree in electrical engineering from Stanford University.

1985 Earns a Ph.D. degree in electrical engineering from Stanford.

1990 Selected by NASA to become an astronaut.

1993 Ellen's first space shuttle flight: mission STS-56 *Discovery*.

1994 Second flight: mission STS-66 *Atlantis*.

1999 Third flight: mission STS-96 *Discovery*.

2002 Fourth flight: mission STS-110 *Atlantis*.

Now Works at NASA as deputy director of Flight Crew Operations.

29

☀ Words to Know ☀

co-inventor—An inventor working along with another inventor.

doctorate—The highest college degree. Also called a Ph.D.

master's degree—An advanced college degree.

NASA (National Aeronautics and Space Administration)—The group that runs the United States space program.

optics—The science of light.

physics—The science that studies matter, energy, and motion.

robotic arm—A machine that can work like a human arm to grab and carry things.

satellite—An object sent into space to orbit the earth.

soloist—A person who performs alone.

space shuttle—A spaceship that can be used over and over to carry people and goods into space and back to Earth.

symphony orchestra—A large group of musicians with many instruments playing long musical works.

☀ Learn More ☀

Books

Iverson, Teresa. *Ellen Ochoa*. Chicago, Ill.: Raintree, 2005.

Paige, Joy. *Ellen Ochoa: The First Hispanic Woman in Space*. New York: Rosen Publishing, 2004.

Walker, Pam. *Ellen Ochoa*. Danbury, Conn.: Children's Press, 2001.

Internet Addresses

A short biography from NASA at the Johnson Space Center Web site.
<http://www.jsc.nasa.gov/Bios/htmlbios/ochoa.html>

An interview with Ellen Ochoa.
<http://teacher.scholastic.com/activities/hispanic/ochoatscript.htm>

NASA for Kids.
<http://www.nasa.gov/audience/forkids/home/index.html>

❊ Index ❊